BLACK POWDER SNAPSHOTS

by

HERBERT ARMENT SHERLOCK

COACHWHIP PUBLICATIONS

Greenville, Ohio

Black Powder Snapshots, by Herbert Arment Sherlock
© 2014 Coachwhip Publications
First published 1946.
No claims made on public domain material.

ISBN 1-61646-277-9
ISBN-13 978-1-61646-277-2

CoachwhipBooks.com

PUBLISHER'S FOREWORD

THE format of this book is purposely one of directness and simplicity. It is increasingly recognized that persons having an historical bent must turn for information to quickly-viewed records of human experience. Not for them is exhaustive research into past affairs; that is work for the scholar. To be sure, profound students of events will continue to assemble facts and evaluate them; but a great portion of these efforts will ultimately be reduced to tabloid form—by necessity. History has become, in these days of radar and the atomic bomb, a swift-rising tide of new information that threatens to engulf its chroniclers, and much that now happens will long remain obscure even to the advanced student. Confronted with this state of affairs, there is reason to assume that pictures and a brief text must furnish the whitecaps of information for each historical wave. The present book is calculated to do this, to furnish vivid and remembered snapshots of the crest of one great historical wave, the Era of Black Powder.

Herbert Arment Sherlock, the illustrator and writer of BLACK POWDER SNAPSHOTS, is a modern user of the old black powder firearms and an authority on their use in the early days of America. Due to Mr. Sherlock's active career in art this book is, understandably and happily, one of pictures. Herein he demonstrates the true artist's instinct for causing his drawing to highlight the text-subject in a delightful and wholly characteristic manner. The result: a book to inform and inspire any person—novice or connoisseur.

Mr. Sherlock has made no attempt to present his word-and-picture stories of the American black powder era in strict historical sequence. Rather, he wishes his audience to enjoy the pages in the manner of thumbing through a snapshot album.

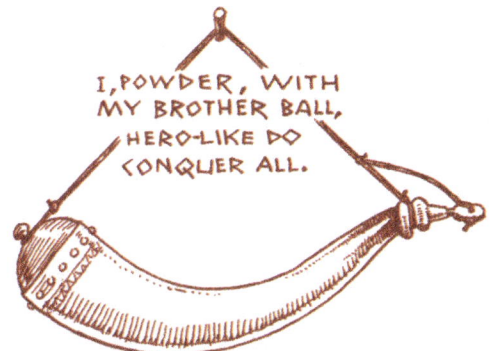

I, POWDER, WITH MY BROTHER BALL, HERO-LIKE DO CONQUER ALL.

HERB SHERLOCK

INVERAWE

THE morning of July 6, 1758, saw an imposing array of fighting men advancing down Lake George toward the French fort of Carillon. In a thousand boats rode 6000 British regulars and 9000 Colonial troops, under the command of General James Abercrombie. Rangers, light infantry, Highlanders, grenadiers and Colonials in their bright and somber uniforms made a colorful spectacle.

Among the Highlanders was one Duncan Campbell of Inverawe, a Major in the Black Watch, or 42nd Highlanders. Several years before the war Campbell had lived in Inverawe House in the Highlands of Western Scotland, where he figured in one of the outstanding ghost stories in history.

Commanding His Majesty's Independent Company of Rangers

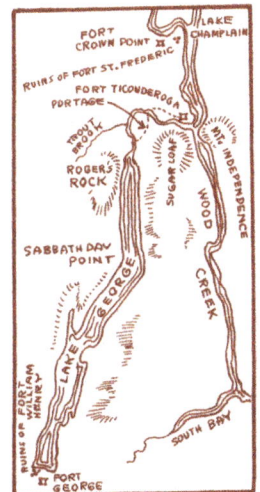

LORD HOWE STONE

MEM. OF Ld HOWE KILLED TROUT BROOK

UNEARTHED AT TICONDEROGA OCT. 1889

It seems that he had hidden a stranger who had confessed to having killed a man, and Campbell swore on his dirk not to reveal him to his pursuers. Then, to Campbell's horror, he learned that the murdered man was his cousin Donald. The next two nights his cousin's ghost appeared to him in dreams and warned him not to conceal the murderer. Finally, on the third night the ghost said farewell to him, but warned him that they would meet again at Ticonderoga.

Campbell later joined the Black Watch. When the regiment came to America and was in the advance on Ticonderoga, he remembered the words of his cousin's ghost about their meeting at that very place. His brother officers told him it was Lake George instead of Ticonderoga, but on the day of battle he insisted the ghost had visited his tent in the night and predicted he would die during the coming attack.

Well, the ghost's prediction did not immediately come true, for Major Campbell was wounded in the arm. The doctors attending him decided to amputate and he died soon after the operation, at Fort Edward, having lived nine days after the battle. His remains lie in Union Cemetery between Fort Edward and Hudson Falls.

Colonial Queen Anne Musket

Length 57 ½ in.   Cal. .75
Barrel 42 in.   Early 1700s

HERB SHERLOCK

SOUTH BARRACKS, FORT TICONDEROGA

FROM Fort Ticonderoga, in the winter of 1776-1777, Mad Anthony Wayne wrote to his friend Benjamin Franklin, "When God made it (if He ever had a hand in it) it was surely done in the dark; it is one confused jumble of stones, without order, beauty or profit."

Here, in 1755, was commenced one of the greatest forts on this continent. Begun that year by Lotbiniere, a French military engineer, the next three years saw the work carried forward with the labor of as many as two thousand men, cutting timbers, quarrying stone and building the outer works and barracks. A sawmill and storehouse were built at the lower falls. The stream was bridged here, and at the head of the portage on Lake George redoubts were built controlling the bridge and landing place there. In the days of Montcalm it was known as Fort Carillon.

In 1758 General James Abercrombie arrived before the fort with 15,000 men and there in front of the French lines was fought one of the costliest battles of the French and Indian War, ending in the defeat of Abercrombie.

The next year Sir Jeffery Amherst laid siege to the fort. The French blew up the powder magazine, then retreated down Lake Champlain and the lilies of France were hauled down for the last time.

Again Ticonderoga was captured, this time by Ethan Allen in 1775, only to be lost two years later to General Burgoyne, as he came over the lake from Canada. Colonel John Brown made a daring but unsuccessful attempt to retake the fort in the fall of the same year. In 1781, when the British abandoned it, the military history of the fort came to a close.

Mr. William F. Pell of New York City leased the property in 1806 and then bought it outright fourteen years later. It has been in the hands of this family ever since.

The south barracks contains the museum, with its priceless relics of French, Colonial and Revolutionary days. The west barracks, the south end of which shows on the left of the drawing, houses the armory on the ground floor. Above, on the second floor, is pointed out the "Ethan Allen door," where that doughty Green Mountain leader demanded the surrender of the fort from Captain Delaplace.

Surely, the preservation of this structure and its contents is a splendid contribution of one family to our country's traditions.

YANKEE DOODLE

HOW HE REALLY LOOKED DURING THE WAR

REVOLUTIONARY WAR ARMY BUTTON

BUCK and BALL

GEN. WASHINGTON'S LOAD — 1 BALL .69 CAL. and 3 BUCKSHOT

French Charleville Musket

Length app. 5 ft.   Cal. .69
Barrel app. 44 in.   Middle 1700s

HERB SHERLOCK

THE PALATINE REGIMENT

ON August 6, 1777, was fought the most sanguinary battle of the Revolution. Redcoat and redskin were pitted against the untrained farmer militia of the Mohawk valley.

In his advance up the valley to the relief of Fort Stanwix, then besieged by St. Leger and the Mohawk chieftain Brant, General Nicholas Herkimer had previously arranged to have a three-gun signal fired from the fort to notify him of the garrison's simultaneously planned attack upon the British camp. While awaiting the signal, Herkimer's officers grew impatient and out of hand. They called him a traitor and a Tory, which was too much for the old gentleman, so he ordered them forward before hearing the signal guns from the fort.

SCALP

The army advanced more like a mob and when but six miles from Stanwix it was ambushed by Brant in a shallow ravine. Herkimer was wounded but continued to direct the fight while sitting under a large tree and calmly smoking his pipe. A heavy thunderstorm interrupted the battle, but when it had abated and fighting begun again, the Indians started to flee as the signal from the fort boomed out. Altho Herkimer held the field, his losses had been so heavy that he could not relieve the fort.

That night the militia buried their dead and then fell back to German Flats. The general was carried home where he lingered 'til the 16th. He passed away in bed while reading the 38th Psalm. Today, in the old Herkimer home, opposite Little Falls, you will find the family Bible lying on a table and beside it the general's sword.

Oriskany is called the bloodiest battle of the Revolution. Just east of the battle monument there is another, dedicated to the four hundred men of Tryon County who fell that memorable August day.

JOSEPH BRANT
(THAYENDANEGEA)

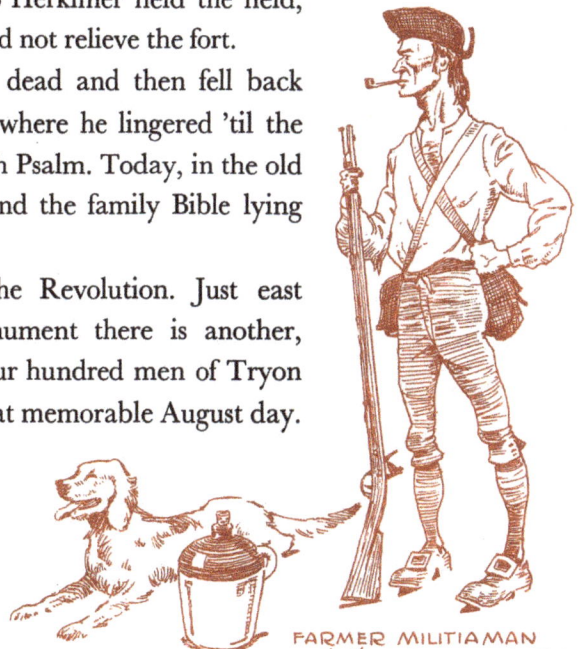

FARMER MILITIAMAN
of the MOHAWK VALLEY

FORT STANWIX
AT ONEIDA STATION
(NOW ROME, NEW YORK)
~ 1777 ~

HERB
SHERLOCK

BEMIS HEIGHTS

IN the second battle of Saratoga, October 7, 1777, Morgan's Corps of Riflemen played a conspicuous part, as they had done previously in the Revolution.

When ordered out to "begin the game," Morgan started from the vicinity of the Neilson house, marched west, circled to the north and then turned back to the east until he contacted the British under General Fraser, who commanded the enemy's right wing. This flanking attack by Morgan hit Fraser as Dearborn and Learned were attacking the British and Hessians near the middle ravine and driving them back. Burgoyne called Fraser back to support these troops, but Fraser's men were being roughly handled by the long rifles.

Morgan grasped the situation at once and ordered several of his men to

NEW YORK
VOLUNTEERS
LOYALIST UNIT

pick off Fraser, as he had great respect for that officer's ability. Just who fired the shot is debatable, but Tim Murphy has been given the credit by most historians. Murphy carried a double-barrel flintlock—one barrel over the other, operating on a common axis, and worked by a lever in front of the trigger guard. Each barrel had its pan and frizzen, with but one hammer to fire both.

The
BRITISH
GRENADIER

Murphy climbed into a tree on a small knoll, from which he could see the British troops milling around to the north of him. And there was Fraser, on a gray horse, attempting to bring order out of chaos. The various historians say the distance between the two men was anywhere from 40 yards to 400. Tim Murphy fired two shots and Fraser knew he was the target of some rifleman, but he had to rally the right wing to prevent disaster. Came a third puff of smoke from the tree in which Murphy sat and Fraser fell mortally wounded, to die the next day and be interred on his last battlefield.

Maybe it was Tim Murphy who fired the fatal shot at General Fraser from the over and under Kentucky rifle, and maybe not. At least, historians agree on some points of the episode—namely that the bullet which killed Fraser was fired by one of the riflemen of Morgan's corps; that the ball came from an over and under Kentucky rifle, and that this shot was probably the turning point of the Revolutionary War. It was shortly after this that France recognized that America was winning and came to her aid against Britain.

BRITISH
ARMY BUTTONS

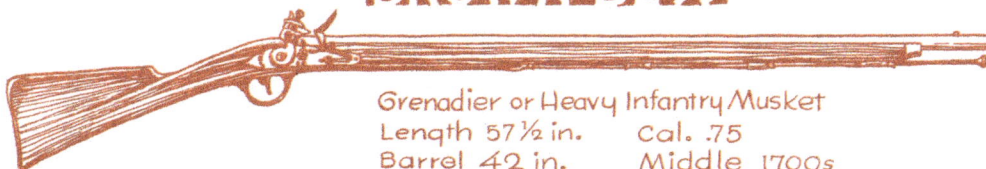

Grenadier or Heavy Infantry Musket
Length 57½ in.   Cal. .75
Barrel 42 in.   Middle 1700s

HERB SHERLOCK

THE BLUFF

NEAR the present town of Bolivar, Ohio, on the banks of the Tuscarawas River, called Muskingum in the old days, stood Fort Laurens, a square structure which enclosed about one acre of land. Here were the conventional blockhouses at each corner, and inside were several log buildings housing officers, men and supplies. It had been built in 1778 by the order of General Lachlan McIntosh to protect the Crossing Place of the Muskingum on the Great Trail, which ran from Fort Pitt, across the Ohio country, to Fort Detroit.

The General also hoped the fort would guard the frontier against Indian raids. It really did help to save the outlying districts, as the Indians were attracted to it like flies to a picnic.

The winter of 1778-79 was an especially cold and bitter one. The men in the fort had been on reduced rations for some time, for besieging the garrison was a force of several hundred Indians from Detroit. No relief had come from Fort Pitt and a couple of men had already been killed attempting to get through the enemy's lines.

Time dragged on and rations grew less; but Colonel John Gibson, in command, was a man of great courage and resourcefulness. One day several Indians, under a flag of truce, demanded food from the fort. Gibson diagnosed the case perfectly. Certainly, he could supply his enemies with food, as the garrison had plenty! He turned over several barrels to the Indians, regardless of the immediate cost to his own men. He had guessed right, for the redskins soon gave up the siege of the fort, thinking that the occupants were too well supplied to be starved into submission.

Fort Laurens was the only military post built by the Continental government during the Revolution within the boundaries of the present state of Ohio.

WYANDOT

UNWELCOME VISITOR
from DETROIT

CAMP KETTLE

OHIO
FLINT ARROWHEAD

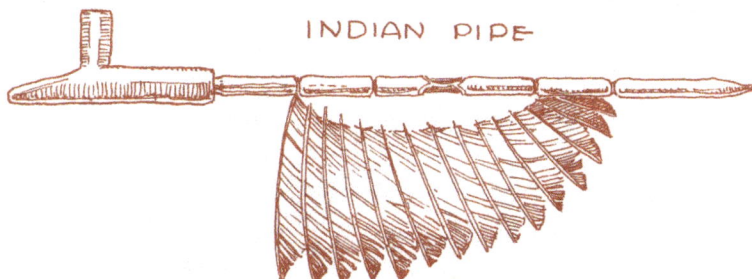

INDIAN PIPE

HERB SHERLOCK

RAIDERS IN THE VALLEY

REDSKINNED SNIPER

FROM the time that the first white man took a shot at a prowling Indian, there were "raiders in the valley." The Indian naturally resented the encroachment of the white settler on his domain and he knew but one way to oust him. New England, New York, Pennsylvania, Ohio, Kentucky, Tennessee— all frontier communities, knew the war whoop, tomahawk, fire-arrow and leaden ball of the raider.

The Indian usually did not have the patience to lay siege to the frontier home, but sought to catch the occupants by surprise. If he were successful in this, the whole family might be toma-

The OLD OAKEN BUCKET

hawked or taken captive. The pioneer cabin was built sturdy and strong, but its weakness lay in fire. If warned beforehand, the owners usually fled to the nearest fort for protection. In Pontiac's war the whole frontier was laid in ashes and the Indians even captured several forts by strategy.

The pioneer, working in his clearing, always had his long rifle handy. Water from the spring, near which he built his cabin, was kept inside for drinking and to put out fire. If the settler was out in the field and was lucky enough not to be cut off from the house, he could put up a good fight from that shelter. The long rifle spelled death to any savage foe who showed too much of his hide from behind a tree or stump. During an attack the women molded bullets and loaded any spare weapons, while the small children usually hugged the floor under the family bed, if a luxury such as a bed was owned. Many a cabin door on the frontier bore the marks of the tomahawk, and many a Red Man fell before those doors while attempting to batter his way inside. The pioneer marksman's Kentucky rifle frequently found its target.

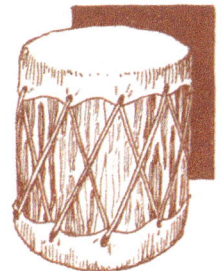

INDIAN DRUM

HERB SHERLOCK

THE EXECUTIONER

THE rites of the False Face Society were first introduced into the Iroquois Nation sometime after 1700. It was a religious society and dealt with the expulsion of evil spirits, though not of the firewater variety.

When the simple rites took place, several warriors in masks would burst into an Indian home. They would question the children, take up ashes from the fireplace and cast them about and look into each corner of the building, shaking turtle or horn rattles all the time to frighten away evil spirits. Today this ritual is still carried on, but the masked men travel from home to home in automobiles.

One of our prominent authors has written a very interesting fictional story based on General Sullivan's march into the Indian country of the Finger Lake region of New York State.* In it he describes a scene taking place in the Indian village of Catherine's Town. The chief priest of the Senecas is calling upon his white captive Sorceress to interpret the dreams of several of his dancing girls. Standing a short distance from the Sorceress is the executioner, face painted black, bow drawn back, awaiting the signal from the high priest to loose his flint-tipped arrow should the Sorceress' interpretations displease the priest.

The Iroquois Confederacy was the most advanced of any Indian confederation upon this continent. Theirs was truly an empire, and one that was feared more than any other by the forest Indians. It reached westward into the Ohio country, some of the Ohio tribes being branches of the original Five Nations, which consisted of the Mohawks, Oneidas, Onondagas, Senecas and Cayugas. Later this confederation was known as the Six Nations, when the Tuscaroras joined it.

*"The Hidden Children," by Robert W. Chambers; D. Appleton & Company, publisher.

The SIX NATIONS

MOHAWKS   ONONDAGAS
SENECAS   CAYUGAS
ONEIDAS   TUSCARORAS

Great Belt of the Confederacy, symbolizing the Gayănessha gowă as an evergrowing tree.

EMPIRE of the SIX NATIONS

HERB SHERLOCK

"TO THE DEATH"

"TO the death" marked the constant struggle between the white man and red man in this country, for the Indian visioned the destruction of the forests, the killing of the game and the expulsion of his people from their fertile valleys and beautiful rivers.

From the time of the first settlements in New England, Virginia and elsewhere the white man began the push that eventually led him across the Appalachians, the Mississippi, the Great Plains, the Rockies—and on to the Pacific Coast. Wherever he hunted and built his home or fort, his every move was contested by the red man.

The use of firearms for the first time by Champlain awed his adversaries, the Iroquois, but the Indians soon rectified this inequality by getting trade guns of their own from the English. These guns were not of the best quality, and were usually muskets of large bore. On the advent of the Kentucky rifle the Indian collected many of these by the simple expedient of catching the owner off guard and lifting his scalp, thereby coming into possession of the coveted firearm. Captain Dillon's book, *The Kentucky Rifle,* contains the picture of Indian Chief Schickellimy's rifle. It was said to have been made for Conrad Weiser, who traded it to the chief for the 'Isle of Q' in the Susquehanna river.

Pontiac brought the Indians together in one great effort to drive the white men from the forests. He organized the Indians of the midwest and succeeded in carrying fire and death to the frontier, but his enemy was too well established and the struggle could have but one ending.

WESTWARD THE PATH OF EMPIRE LEADS

MOUNTAIN MAN

The PACIFIC

THE END OF THE TRAIL

BIG
TURKEY SHOOT

NOVEMBER 15 & 16

TO BE HELD AT
ENSIGN'S CLEARING.

EVERYBODY WELCOME!
HUNTERS, TRAPPERS,
TRADERS COME AND
BRING YOUR FRIENDS.

ALL SHOOTING AT
60 YARDS OFFHAND.
LIVE TURKEYS.

FLINTS, KNIVES, POWDER
& GUN REPAIRING.

L. ENSIGN.
GUNSMITH

"GIT YORESELF A RIFLED GUN, MISTER, AN' GIT AQUAINTED WITH UT."

HERB SHERLOCK

SHOOTIN' MATCH

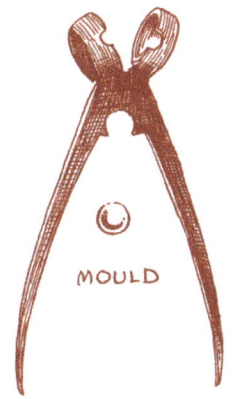

MOULD

EACH individual has his own ideas as to which position he likes best in shooting at targets; also, the type of target in which to punch holes. Maybe it will be prone with the barrel resting on a log; maybe from a bench, or, just standing on his "hind legs." There is usually an argument about which position shows a person's real shooting ability. However, a target is generally regarded as such as long as the human eye can see it distinctly.

FLINTS

Back in Colonial days when the old Brown Bess, Queen Anne and Charleville muskets were all the vogue and the product and fame of the Pennsylvania gunsmiths had not yet made their appearance in many places, a shooting match between men using these big smoothbores was nothing "to write home about." Bullet patches were unknown, and the naked ball did not lend itself to accuracy. Let's look at our illustration.

FRIZZEN PICK

MAIN-SPRING VISE

Now, into the group gathered at the local tavern for a turkey shoot, stroll two men dressed in buckskin. They are strangers and are "jest passin' through." The landlord, with an eye to business, suggests they stop and try their luck. They do not hesitate, after taking a squint at the muskets being used by the other contestants. When their turn comes they toss in their shillings and load their long rifles. The local rustics gape at those guns—the beauty of the curly maple stocks and the patch boxes, artistically designed and engraved. They watch the hunters prime the pans, pour a powder charge down the barrel, then place a buckskin patch on the muzzle with a ball in the center. At once everyone starts to ask questions, as no one has ever seen this done before, but each rifleman calmly completes his loading and steps up in his turn to fire at the target.

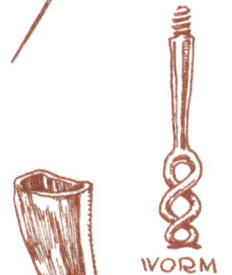

WORM

HORN POWDER MEASURE

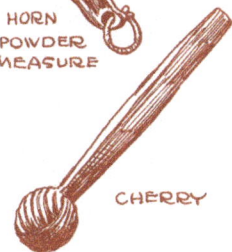

CHERRY

The picture tells the rest of the story, and by the looks on the faces of the losers one can easily surmise that the coming of the Kentucky Rifle created a new branch in the family of guns for war and target.

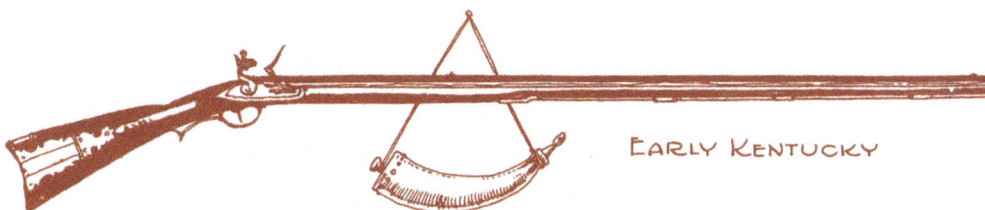

EARLY KENTUCKY

HERB SHERLOCK

"PALAVER"

IT is said that the Indians liked to hear the sing-song French which the voyageurs and coureur de bois spoke, better than the harsh tones of our English forbears. Or, perhaps, their regard for the French was enhanced by the brand of firewater the French passed around, to spread their influence across Lake Ontario and down the Allegheny, Ohio and Mississippi rivers.

However, the English didn't do too badly either. Sir William Johnson made quite a name for himself as Superintendent of Indian Affairs for North America. At Johnson Hall, Johnstown, New York, the big elm and lilacs are pointed out to the visitor today, where Sir William held his councils with his red brethren.

Either PEACE or WAR

On the frontier, the trader came to swap bright cloth, beads, pans and other items for furs. If the Indian wanted a gun, and he usually did, the trader would have an extra long one, because the beaver skins stacked beside that musket had to reach as high as the gun was long, and the longer it was the more beaver pelts the trader received.

Whatever the trade was for it took a lot of "palaver" (talk) and this the Indian loved, as he was a born orator. Guns were placed on the ground in front of their owners and each group sat in an arc behind the spokesman. At the conclusion of the "palaver" the pipe was passed to each man. No one was supposed to violate the proceedings of a council, but tradition was sometimes shattered when whiskey was mixed with words, for then the trouble started.

ME GETTUM SKINNED, NOT BEAVER!

MILITARY
.69 CAL.

18 BALLS
TO POUND

KENTUCKY
.47 CAL.

48 BALLS
TO POUND

KENTUCKY FLINT PISTOL

DANIEL BOONE

1734 - 1820

HERB SHERLOCK

DANIEL BOONE

NO history of black powder could be complete without a word about Daniel Boone, the master of the wilderness. He was born in Oley Township, now Berks County, Pennsylvania, and died at his son Nathan's home in Missouri, but his name and fame will ever be coupled with the history of Kentucky.

Boone was first a master hunter and Indian fighter, for he knew his red brothers as no other knew them. They liked and admired him, even adopting him into the tribe (Shawnee) after his capture at a salt lick.

The picture of Boone here reproduced was drawn from a painting by Chester Harding. Artist Harding painted it in Missouri, when Boone was eighty-four. He was infirm at the time, but related many anecdotes of his early life to the painter. It was at this time that, in answer to the question if he had ever been lost, Boone replied, "No, I can't say as ever I was lost, but I was bewildered once for three days." Soon after the portrait was finished Boone passed on. It seems that Daniel, his father and his grandfather, to say nothing of his sons, all belonged to the Itching Foot clan. They did not care for crowds, and Daniel, especially, always wanted more "elbow room."

As one looks at his portrait and sees the deep-set eyes, firm lips and lower jaw, and high forehead crowned by long white hair, there comes the feeling that the character of Daniel Boone was well written into his every feature.

SIGNATURE OF BOONE
IN THE YEAR 1784

HUNTING BAG *and*
POWDERHORN

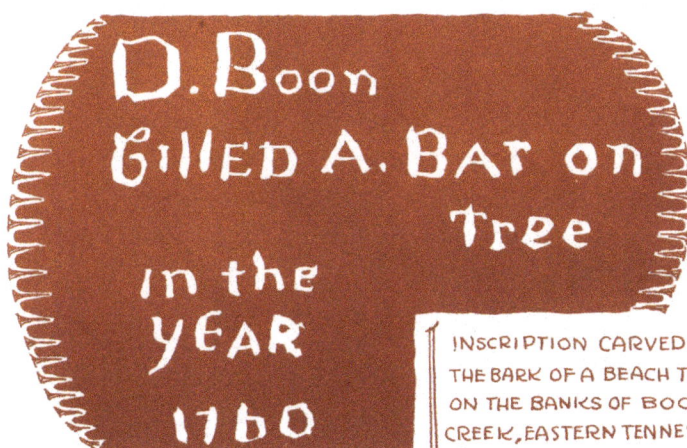

D. Boon
killed A. Bar on
Tree
in the
Year
1760

INSCRIPTION CARVED IN
THE BARK OF A BEACH TREE
ON THE BANKS OF BOON'S
CREEK, EASTERN TENNESSEE.
from DANIEL BOONE BY JOHN BAKELESS.

HERB
SHERLOCK

THE WILDERNESS ROAD

The SAFEST PORT IN A
FRONTIER STORM

LET us turn back the pages of history to the days when the crossing of the Alleghenies was a new and perilous undertaking. The roads were mere ruts cut through the wilderness, but they led one ever westward toward the "promised land."

Try and put yourself in the place of the pioneer. You have packed everything you own into the Conestoga wagon, which will be the family home until you reach the Ohio country. Clothing, furniture, bedding and the two most necessary articles for frontier life—the long rifle and the ax. The rifle will supply the meat for the table and the ax will hew out a clearing and cut the logs for the cabin.

Behind the team of oxen the huge springless wagon, with its flapping canvas top, bumps and groans over the rutted roads. There are no soft-cushioned seats for mother and the children to ride on, and the jarring jolts from stones or holes in the road make the riders' bones and muscles ache. Brother Samuel rides the only horse, and it is his job to scout for signs of Red Men looking for easy plunder. He must also select the next camp site where water can be found.

Day after day you goad your ox team on, down wilderness roads hardly as wide as the Conestoga, cross rivers by ferry until finally you reach Fort Pitt at the junction of the Allegheny and Monongahela rivers. After a short rest you push on down the Ohio towards Fort Steuben.

Forests cover hill and bottom land alike—this is Ohio, the promised land. Here you will clear your land, build your cabin and raise your family, as thousands more have done in the years past. Some day, as you stand in your doorway, many of the huge Conestoga wagons—and later the prairie schooners—will pass, each pushing farther westward to found a nation that will stretch from the Atlantic to the Pacific.

COLONIAL
LANTERNS

POWDER
KEG

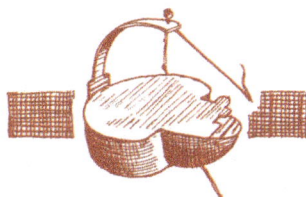

BETTY LAMP

CANDLE
MOLD

"THE OLD SOW"

H ARDLY the appropriate name for an old cannon that helped win a battle, but the men of Sackett's Harbor had so called it and the name stuck.

It was the year 1812 and the Harbor was the scene of intense activity, as the word had come that Commodore Earle, the British naval commander on Lake Ontario, was heading into the bay from Kingston across the lake. "The Old Sow" had been intended for the brig Oneida, but, as it was a 32-pounder, it was found to be too heavy for the ship. This cannon had then been left on the beach—like an old sow, to wallow in the mud. In a frenzied attempt to put the fortifications in readiness for the impending attack, "the Old Sow" was raised from its resting place and given a dignified position in a small six-foot earthworks.

When the British fleet finally made its appearance, the line of battle was led by the Royal George, 24 guns. Slowly the enemy bore down, bringing his guns to bear on the small forts. In the excitement, no one had noticed that "the Old Sow," a 32-pounder, would require a larger ball than the other defending pieces, 24-pounders. This presented a problem to the gunners, as they had no 32-pound cannon balls. They tried to solve it by wrapping rags and petticoats around the smaller balls, but the accuracy just wasn't there.

The solution of a proper ball for "the Old Sow" came from the Royal George. A 32-pound ball from the flagship buried itself in the earthworks surrounding "the Old Sow" and this was immediately dug out and rammed down her throat. Careful aim was taken, she belched a cloud of smoke, and a shower of timbers was seen to rise from the stern of the Royal George. Afterward, it was learned that 14 of the enemy seamen had been killed and 18 wounded. "The Old Sow's" bite had equaled her grunt.

ONE OF HARRISON'S VETERANS.

BRITISH SEAMAN

The LAST FLINT LOCK - 1840 MODEL

SACKETTS HARBOR · 1812

HERB SHERLOCK

SHARPSHOOTER

IN wars of the past the crackshots of the various regiments or companies were known as sharpshooters. Today they are called snipers. Their duties have always been much the same, although in black powder days a sharpshooter had to change his position more often because the cloud of white smoke from the discharge of his gun revealed his hiding place to his enemy, who were liable to throw a few cannon balls his way.

The story is told by Sawyer of a certain captain in the Union forces, who was a very fine shot. He, with several aides, built a de luxe sniper's nest opposite the enemy's camp. They "doped out" the angle-of-fire, wind-drift and even the length of time it would take the bullet to reach its mark. When the opportunity came to fire, the captain picked as his target the senior officer of three who were grouped around a table studying a map. As he squeezed the trigger of his heavy target rifle, which was equipped with a telescope, the commanding general of the enemy force stepped out of a tent near the table and started toward the officers. As he approached the group, the men got to their feet, one of them accidentally stepping on a map that had slipped to the ground. He moved over a pace, the general passed him and received the bullet intended for the staff officer. Now, the facts on this remarkable shot are: it took four and three-quarters seconds for the bullet to reach its mark, and the distance was one mile and one hundred and eighty-seven feet!

Among the famous sharpshooter regiments in the Civil War was Berdan's. There were two regiments formed, and their crackshots came from eight different states. From the spring of 1862 to the end of the war these men carried Sharps rifles through many of the hardest-fought battles of the conflict.

PRIVATE IN THE FAMOUS BERDAN SHARPSHOOTERS

FEDERAL U·S BELT BUCKLE

SHARPSHOOTER

HERB SHERLOCK

SKIRMISHER IN GRAY

ALWAYS opposite the line in blue was the gray-clad skirmisher of the South. From Bull Run to Appomattox he was in the forefront of every battle, contacting the enemy, feeling out their strength and bearing the brunt of first fire. Despite his torn clothing, worn-out shoes and scarcity of food and ammunition this man in gray traded blow for blow for his beloved Lee.

ROBERT E. LEE

At Gettysburg, the Confederate advance swept to the high ground in front of Round Top. Just beyond was Little Round Top, the key to the Union position. The Confederates attacked with an outflanking line at four o'clock in the afternoon. Vincent threw his brigade into their path and a hand-to-hand struggle took place for Little Round Top. In the conflict which ensued the Confederates were forced from the hill. From the rocky ground in front of the position, called the Devil's Den, came a deadly fire that swept the Union line. Artillery from Round Top poured shot and shell into the place, for already General Vincent was dead, General Weed wounded and Colonel O'Rourke and Lieutenant Hazlett killed. When the fighting was over, a Confederate skirmisher was found dead from a wound in the head, caused by a shell fragment. He had built a rifle-pit by piling up smaller stones between two huge rocks and from this improvised fort he probably had accounted for more than one Union officer.

C.S.A.

CONFEDERATE BELT BUCKLE

Perhaps this skirmisher in our picture was lucky enough to escape the leaden hail through four years of warfare. He finally cherished, as his only reward, the memory of having been with Stonewall Jackson at Bull Run or with Lee in the Wilderness.

HERB SHERLOCK

STORMING THE REDOUBT

THE order has come to advance on the enemy's position, the center of which is a strongly held redoubt. Several cannon frown down upon the line of blue and soon grape and canister will whistle and tear through the ranks. In the center of the attacking line is a Zouave regiment in bright uniforms, splendid targets for the enemy. They advance; the guns open fire, and powder-smoke shrouds the whole front of the redoubt. Bullets and shells find their mark and men fall, but the ranks close up and rush on. The grim survivors lower their bayonets and make the final charge, up and over the top, and the colors are quickly planted on the parapet.

Even as late as the Civil War we find picturesque uniforms worn into battle and of these the ones worn by the Fire Zouaves were the most colorful.

COLONEL ELMER E. ELLSWORTH

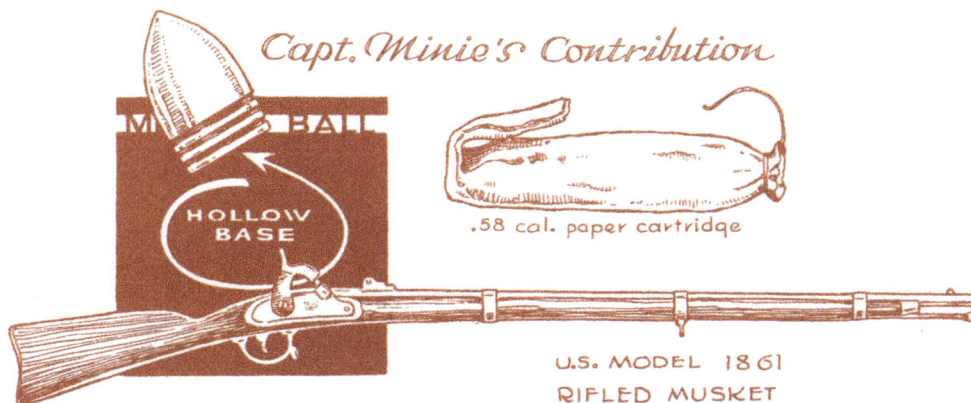

WARRIOR DE LUXE

There were a number of these Zouave regiments attired in gaudy Algerian dress and one of the most noted was that under the command of Colonel Elmer E. Ellsworth.

In May of 1861, Ellsworth's regiment was included in a movement of troops across the Potomac, toward Alexandria, Virginia. When they entered that town a Confederate flag was seen flying over the Marshall House, a local hotel. Colonel Ellsworth went to the roof and removed it, but as he was descending he was fatally shot by the tavern owner, who was in turn killed by Private Francis E. Brownell of the Zouaves.

Capt. Minie's Contribution

MINIE BALL

HOLLOW BASE

.58 cal. paper cartridge

U.S. MODEL 1861 RIFLED MUSKET

HERB SHERLOCK

The DESPATCH RIDER

Oh, whether they be Arapahoes
Or Ogallala Sioux,
    Injuns don't mean a cussed thing,
Fer despatches must go through.

    Up the road from Laramie,
Acrost the Oregon Trail,
    The poundin' o' hoofbeats echo
In answer to the emigrants' hail.

    Beyond old Fort Fetterman,
North o' the Powder an' Clear;
    Hostiles in force on the Big Horn
Gatherin' from far an' near.

GEORGE ARMSTRONG CUSTER
Born Dec. 5, 1839 in
Harrison County, Ohio,
died June 25, 1876 in
the battle of the Little Big
Horn, Montana.

"Custer's yonder to'ards the Yellowstone
An' thar's plenty o' Injun sign."
    Them's the words o' the despatcher
From o'er the Montana line.

    His hoss was plumb tuckered out,
Fer the Injuns had give 'em a run;
    But he only laughed at our questions
An' patted his old Colt gun.

Be it the North Platte or Powder river,
The Chugwater or Buffalo crick;
    It's all the same to them riders—
Fer Injuns they don't care a lick.

    The rain or the sleet may be fallin',
Or the sky overhead a deep blue;
    The trail fairly crawlin' with hostiles,
But the despatches must go through.

Colt Army .44
MODEL OF 1860

HERB SHERLOCK

SCOUT OF FOUR AT BAY

BENT'S FORT on the ARKANSAS
HEADQUARTERS FOR HUNTERS,
TRAPPERS and INDIANS.

"HOLED-UP" in the ruins of an adobe house, three troopers and a scout are fighting for their lives against a band of Comanches on the warpath. The hostiles have made several rushes in efforts to wipe out these men, but have been beaten back at each attempt. Water is getting low and ammunition is almost spent, as the sun slowly sinks toward the western horizon. The men stare through sunken, bloodshot eyes for signs of rescue. The wounded man stirs restlessly and talks to himself. The old scout fires at an unwary Indian and only grunts as he sees the redskin sprawl out on the hot prairie, a hole in his forehead. Suddenly, to the north, the eyes of the scout pick up a

COUP FEATHER

MAYNARD TAPE PRIMER ON 1855 LOCK
1858 U.S. SPRINGFIELD

distant cloud of dust, which is barely discernible to the naked eye, but to a man like himself, accustomed to the western country, he knows it to mark the head of the prayed-for cavalry column.

In the days of the Indian troubles on the plains many a small scouting party was wiped out by the Red Men, when caught in their circle of death. The troopers were armed with the old single-shot Springfield .45-70 carbines, the cavalry standby. It was a good gun—none better as a purely military single-shot breech loader. It had been adopted by the swivel-chair "brass hats" in Washington; but the Indians didn't have an ordnance department, and their proving ground was the field of battle. Gun-running was an old game and the Indians soon found that repeating Spencers, Henrys and Winchesters were much more effective than any single-shot firearm of that day.

Sharp's "Old Reliable"
Caliber .52

HERB SHERLOCK

ACES AND EIGHTS

SHOOTING scrapes were as common as fleas on a dog when the West was still untamed. Cards were a favorite diversion and many a game ended minus one of the players, who soon was placed permanently in the town's "boot hill."

Perhaps one of the players called another a very uncomplimentary name, as did Trampas in Owen Wister's famous novel, *The Virginian*—when in reply to Trampas' particular epithet, the Virginian calmly ordered, "When you call me that, SMILE."

The smoke was so thick you could cut it,
An' the lamp didn't rival no sun;
When the kid with the steel gray eyes
Dropped his hand to the butt of his gun.
"You dealt from the bottom, tin horn—"
Both shots were meant to kill,
But Judge Colt got the decision
And the tin horn got Boot Hill.

LUCKY DAN SLADE
DIED JULY 4, 1876
HE DEALT FROM THE BOTTOM

BOOT HILL

In 1876, in Deadwood, South Dakota, a poker game was in progress in a saloon, when a man walked up behind one of the players and fired a shot into the back of his head. The man who slumped to the floor was that man of the lightning draw, Wild Bill Hickok. Bill didn't have a chance against this cowardly act, but as life left his body his two forty-five Colts were half way out of their holsters, clutched in stiffening fingers.

Many men have died in gunfire at a card table and nothing but a few lines in the local paper's obituary column were ever written or remembered about the incidents, but the poker hand that Wild Bill held when he died has become famous as Aces and Eights, "dead man's hand."

BOWIE KNIFE

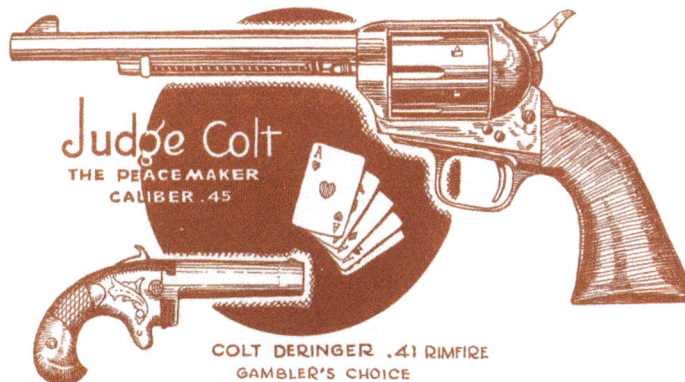

Judge Colt
THE PEACEMAKER
CALIBER .45

COLT DERINGER .41 RIMFIRE
GAMBLER'S CHOICE

HERB SHERLOCK

THE "BUNTLINE SPECIAL"

A FEW years ago, every boy read the stories written by Ned Buntline—tales of the Wild and Woolly West, that featured the exploits of plains scouts, buffalo hunters and frontier marshals. The covers of these novels were often embellished with an action-drawing showing a great scout and a rascally Indian at grips and the pages were crammed with the hero's fabulous accomplishments.

Buntline actually associated with the men he wrote about—Buffalo Bill Cody, Wyatt Earp, Bat Masterson, Billy Tilghman and many others. No doubt the author availed himself of a writer's

WYATT EARP
FRONTIER MARSHAL

The
COLT .45

privilege to invent incidents and otherwise speed the action, and to good effect, for the people "back East" fairly clamored for his product.

The frontier marshals impressed Buntline so favorably that he had a number of Colt Frontier Six Shooters made especially for them, with twelve-inch barrels. Most of the recipients of his gifts soon cut that long barrel down to conventional length, claiming it slowed their draw. Marshal Earp, however, used the gun in its original form. He found the long barrel especially handy in quelling a saloon brawl, as he could slap a man's head with it and render him hors de combat.

another persuader

HERB SHERLOCK

THE GUN COLLECTOR

THE word "collector" covers a large field of activity. Such a hobbyist may collect coins, stamps, buttons, Indian relics, antique furniture and many other articles. Here, we have pictured the gun collector.

Possibly he is a Colt specialist who owns all models from the rare Paterson down to the present-day .45-caliber semi-automatic pistol. Without looking far, we'd find another man who is equally interested in collecting fine old Kentucky "flinters"; and yet another devotes his attention to assembling all models of United States military shoulder weapons, from the 1795 flintlock of .69-caliber to the .30-06 Springfield.

Most firearms bear proof marks and maker's names and dates. These are usually inscribed on the barrel or lock plate, and one of the most interesting phases of gun collecting rests in the process of establishing the gun's identity by means of its original markings. The student of firearms is seldom at a loss to identify his acquisitions, for he can refer to books on the subject, speak to fellow collectors, or, where much obscurity is involved, seek the advice of the curators of great arms collections.

So, in leaving our collector friend, we note the smile upon his face and the appraising way in which he fondles that pistol. We can almost hear a faint sigh of pleasure as he visualizes his "item" in the midst of a battle on the Spanish Main. He dreams—even as you and I!

BRITISH FLINT
BLUNDERBUS
COACH PISTOL
with SPRING BAYONET under BARREL
PERIOD of 1760

REMINGTON
NAVY BREECH-
LOADING PISTOL
Model of 1867
CALIBER .50

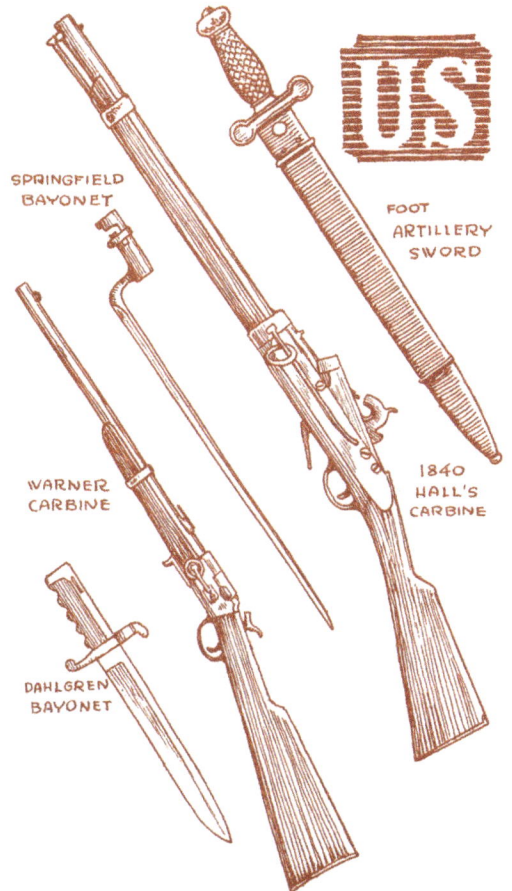

SPRINGFIELD
BAYONET

US

FOOT
ARTILLERY
SWORD

WARNER
CARBINE

1840
HALL'S
CARBINE

DAHLGREN
BAYONET

.34 CALIBER
TEXAS
PATERSON

GUN COLLECTOR means
MUSKETS, MUSKETOONS, RIFLES,
CARBINES, PISTOLS, REVOLVERS,
BAYONETS and associate items.

• 5 SHOTS
and
CONCEALED TRIGGER.

• MADE IN DIFFERENT LENGTHS OF BARREL
and
FURNISHED WITH TWO TYPES OF STOCKS,
The REGULAR PATERSON STOCK and the
STRAIGHT STOCK.

OFFHAND

HERB SHERLOCK

MUZZLE-LOADING RIFLE MATCHES

EVER since Goliath served as David's target, men have been demonstrating their marksmanship on wood, paper, tin cans and each other.

During the early days of this country, flintlock and percussion rifles were used in shooting matches, as shooting-accuracy then meant meat on the table and successful defense of the frontier—in short, the difference between life and death. Today, we find those same old rifles and newer ones of

similar design punching holes in paper targets for a host of devoted black powder shooters. Modern smokeless powder rifles will never push the old "coal burners" off the target range or hunting trail as long as Americans have pride and lively interest in their country's beginnings.

Summer and winter, the modern shooters of black powder guns are on their target ranges, hard at work making the historic guns shoot "tens," swapping ideas and enjoying life in general. The competition in this game is very keen and often the bullet-hole which is only slightly off-center does not win the match. It really takes a pinwheel to sew up a match!

In tournaments, each match calls for a certain number of shots to be fired with a round ball or slug gun at a specified range and in one of the four customary shooting positions pictured on the following pages. The remarkable accuracy attained with these rifles is well worth any "gun-bug's" study.

SCHUETZEN STYLE

The slug gun pictured here fires an elongated bullet of pure lead, which is swaged beforehand for uniformity. Narrow paper strips are placed cross-like on a false muzzle for patching. A bullet-starter forces the slug carefully into the barrel and the ramrod is then used to complete the seating of the bullet on the powder.

These rifles are usually heavy and very accurate at ranges of 100 and 220 yards. Most marksmen use a telescope or tube sight for fine sighting.

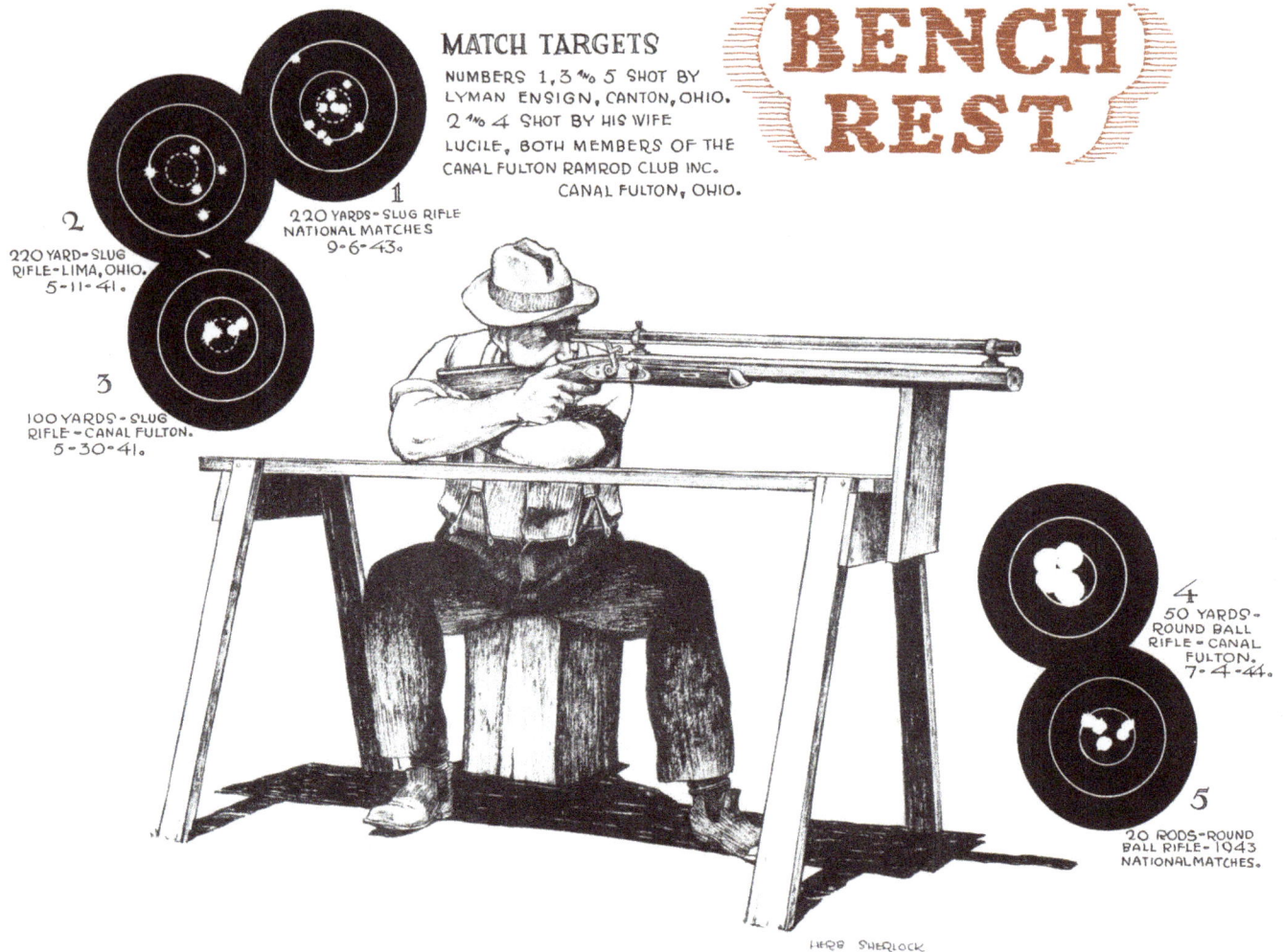

MATCH TARGETS

NUMBERS 1, 3 AND 5 SHOT BY
LYMAN ENSIGN, CANTON, OHIO.
2 AND 4 SHOT BY HIS WIFE
LUCILE, BOTH MEMBERS OF THE
CANAL FULTON RAMROD CLUB INC.
CANAL FULTON, OHIO.

BENCH REST

2
220 YARD-SLUG
RIFLE-LIMA, OHIO.
5-11-41.

1
220 YARDS-SLUG RIFLE
NATIONAL MATCHES
9-6-43.

3
100 YARDS-SLUG
RIFLE-CANAL FULTON.
5-30-41.

4
50 YARDS-
ROUND BALL
RIFLE-CANAL
FULTON.
7-4-44.

5
20 RODS-ROUND
BALL RIFLE-1943
NATIONAL MATCHES.

HERB SHERLOCK

Scoring of a target is by string measurement from the center of the bullet hole to the center of the target. This gives no advantage to the large bore guns over their smaller competitors. The National Rifle Association small bore rifle targets are in general use everywhere.

The Canal Fulton Ramrod Club of Ohio, situated on State Route 21, which parallels the historic Ohio-Erie Canal, is the oldest club of its kind in the country, shooting matches having been held here since 1812.

NOW, I ASK YOU ONE AND ALL, MY FRIENDS,
TO TAKE A LONG AND CAREFUL LOOK;
WHY AM I CHOSEN AS THE TAIL-PIECE
TO END THIS LITTLE BOOK?

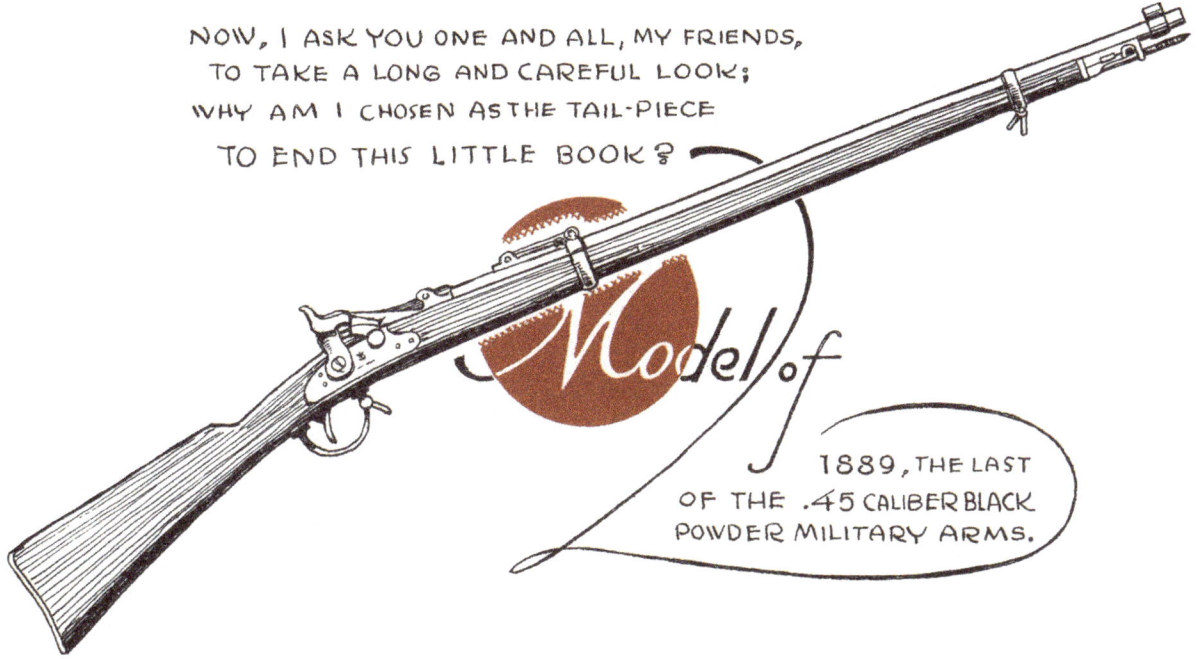

Model of

1889, THE LAST
OF THE .45 CALIBER BLACK
POWDER MILITARY ARMS.

COACHWHIP PUBLICATIONS

COACHWHIPBOOKS.COM

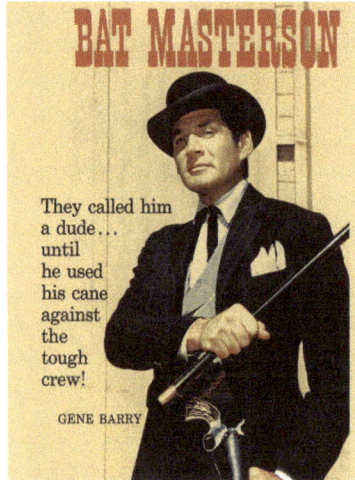

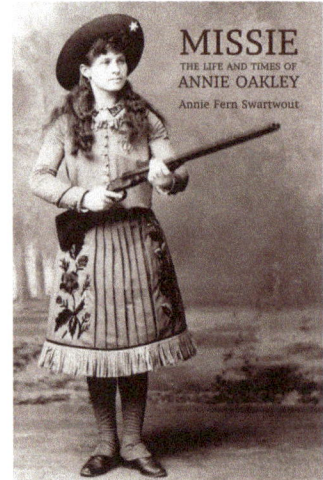

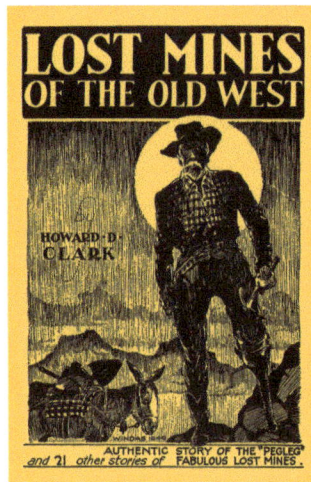

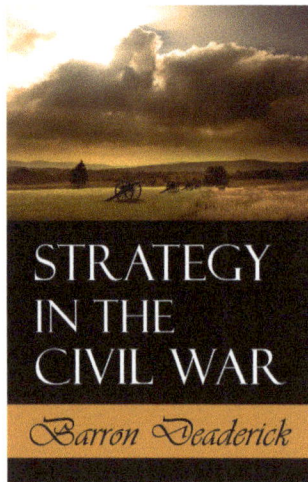

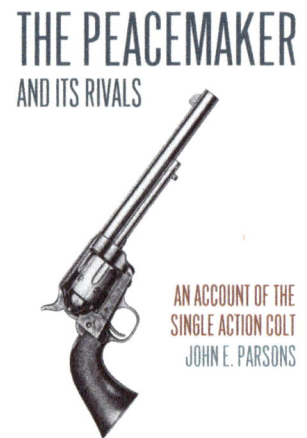

PRIMITIVE AND PIONEER SPORTS
FOR RECREATION TODAY

Bernard S. Mason

BAT MASTERSON

They called him a dude... until he used his cane against the tough crew!

GENE BARRY

MISSIE
THE LIFE AND TIMES OF ANNIE OAKLEY

Annie Fern Swartwout

LOST MINES
OF THE OLD WEST

HOWARD D. CLARK

AUTHENTIC STORY OF THE "PEGLEG"
and 21 other stories of FABULOUS LOST MINES.

STRATEGY IN THE CIVIL WAR

Barron Deaderick

THE PEACEMAKER
AND ITS RIVALS

AN ACCOUNT OF THE
SINGLE ACTION COLT
JOHN E. PARSONS

COACHWHIP PUBLICATIONS

ALSO AVAILABLE

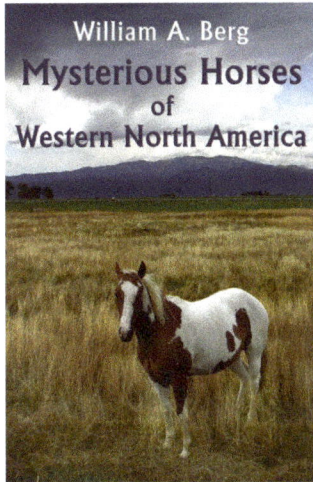

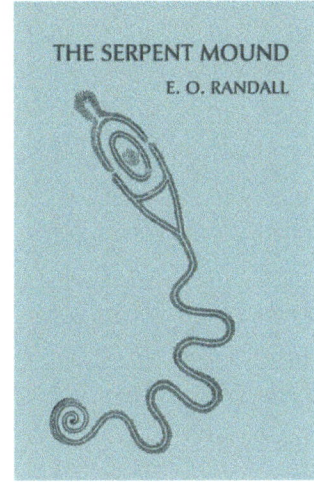

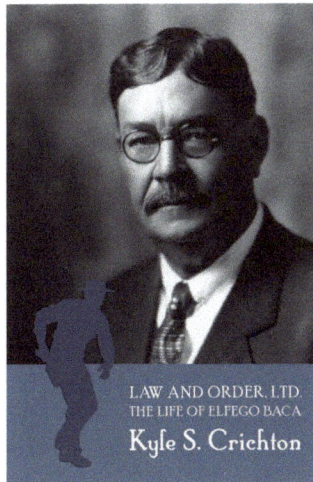

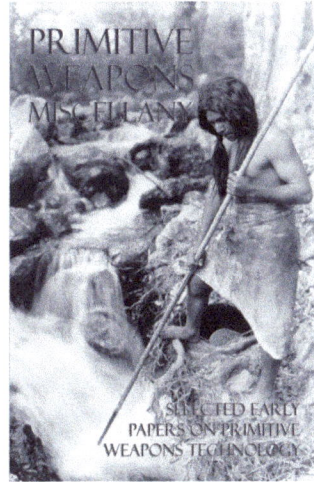

William A. Berg
Mysterious Horses
of
Western North America

DRUMS, TOMTOMS, AND RATTLES

BERNARD S. MASON

THE SERPENT MOUND
E. O. RANDALL

LAW AND ORDER, LTD.
THE LIFE OF ELFEGO BACA
Kyle S. Crichton

HOW TO DRAW HORSES
JOHN SKEAPING

PRIMITIVE
WEAPONS
MISCELLANY

SELECTED EARLY
PAPERS ON PRIMITIVE
WEAPONS TECHNOLOGY